T0390027

SLITHERING SNAKES

Rat Snakes

by Joanne Mattern

BLASTOFF! READERS 2

BELLWETHER MEDIA • MINNEAPOLIS, MN

Blastoff! Readers are carefully developed by literacy experts to build reading stamina and move students toward fluency by combining standards-based content with developmentally appropriate text.

Level 1 provides the most support through repetition of high-frequency words, light text, predictable sentence patterns, and strong visual support.

Level 2 offers early readers a bit more challenge through varied sentences, increased text load, and text-supportive special features.

Level 3 advances early-fluent readers toward fluency through increased text load, less reliance on photos, advancing concepts, longer sentences, and more complex special features.

★ **Blastoff! Universe**

Reading Level

Grade K

Grades 1–3

Grade 4

This edition first published in 2026 by Bellwether Media, Inc.

No part of this publication may be reproduced in whole or in part without written permission of the publisher. For information regarding permission, write to Bellwether Media, Inc., Attention: Permissions Department, 3500 American Blvd W, Suite 150, Bloomington, MN 55431.

Library of Congress Cataloging-in-Publication Data

LC record for Rat Snakes available at: https://lccn.loc.gov/2025001566

Editor: Kieran Downs   Designer: Brittany McIntosh

Printed in the United States of America, North Mankato, MN.

Table of Contents

Meet the Rat Snake

eastern rat snake

Rat snakes are **reptiles**. There are about 50 different **species** of rat snakes.

They live in North America, Europe, and eastern Asia.

Eastern Rat Snake Range

N
W   E
S

range =

Rat snakes come in different sizes. Most rat snakes are around 5 feet (1.5 meters) long.

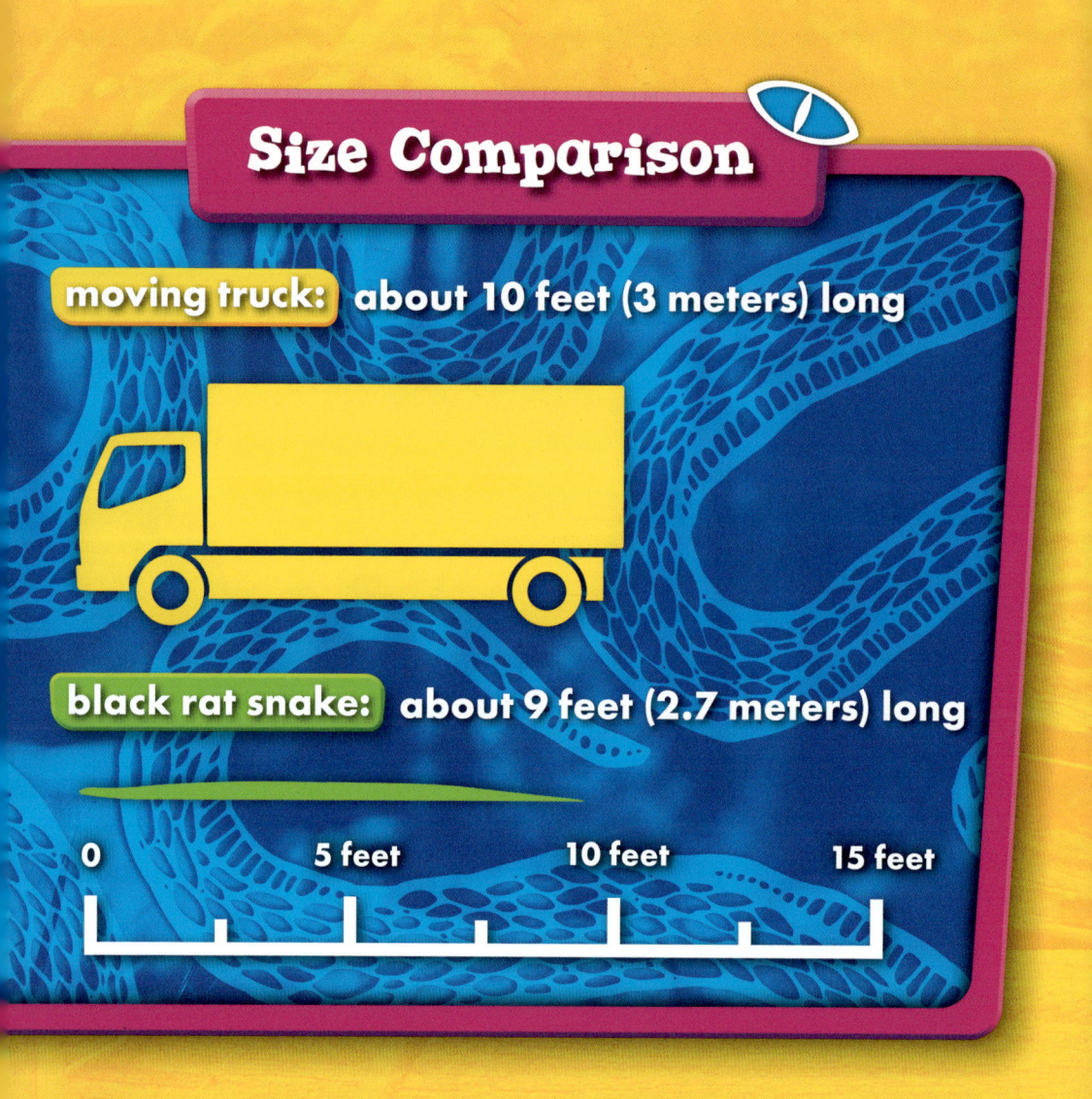

Size Comparison

moving truck: about 10 feet (3 meters) long

black rat snake: about 9 feet (2.7 meters) long

0   5 feet   10 feet   15 feet

black
rat snake

Some are up to 9 feet
(2.7 meters) long!

Baird's rat snake

The color of rat snakes varies by species and where they live. They can be black, red, yellow, or green.

8

Some rat snakes only have one color. Others have many.

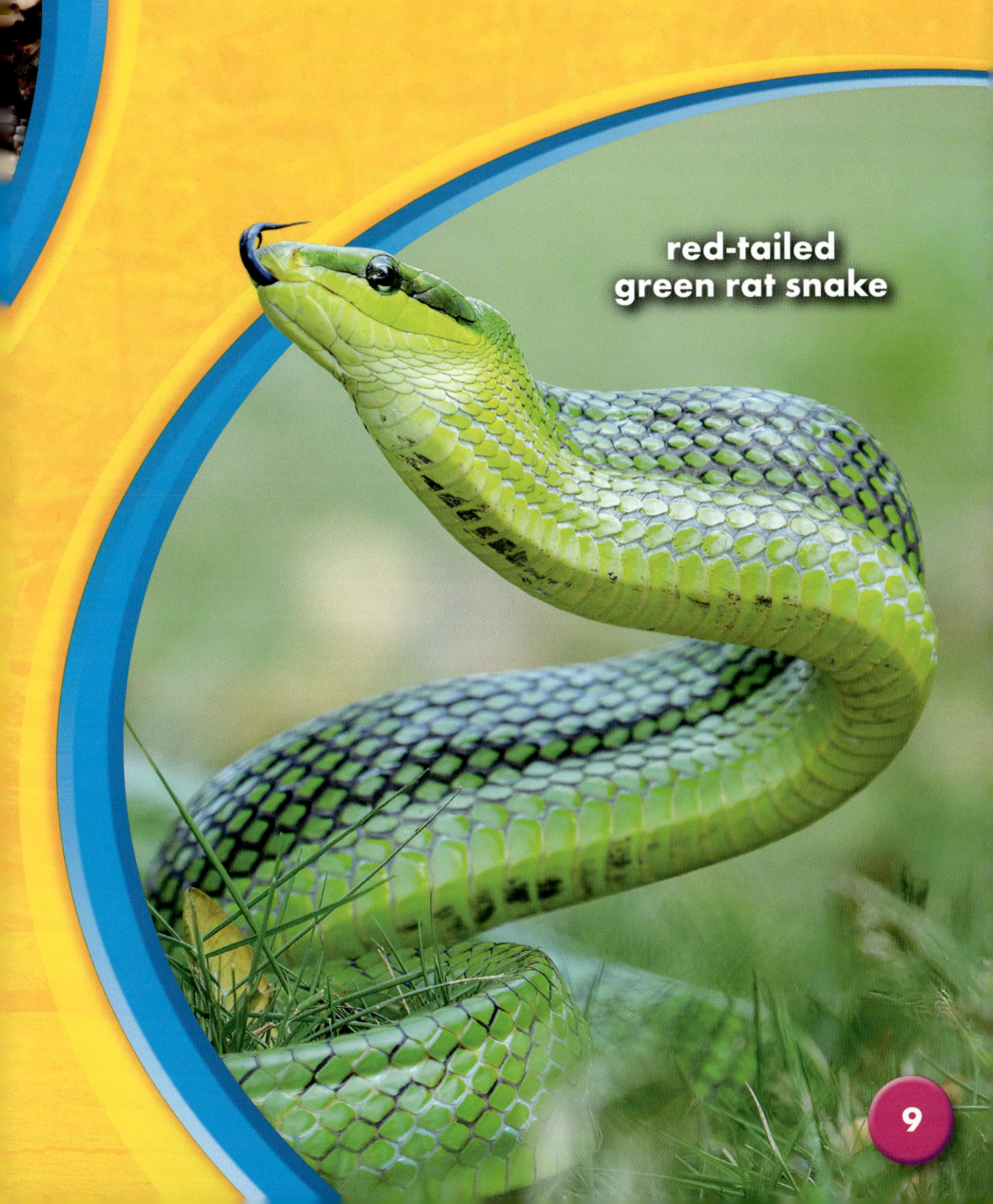

red-tailed green rat snake

snout

Rat snakes have rounded **snouts**. They also have round eyes.

A **ridge** runs down the middle of rat snakes' **scales**.

Spot a Rat Snake!

round eyes

rounded snout

ridged scales

Hunting and Squeezing

Rat snakes live in forests and **grasslands**. They are great at climbing.

The snakes eat rats. This is where they got their name. They also eat frogs and small **rodents**.

Rat Snake Food

American bullfrogs

house rats

house mice

Rat snakes are **constrictors**. They tightly **wrap** their bodies around their **prey**.

14

The prey stops breathing. The snakes swallow meals whole.

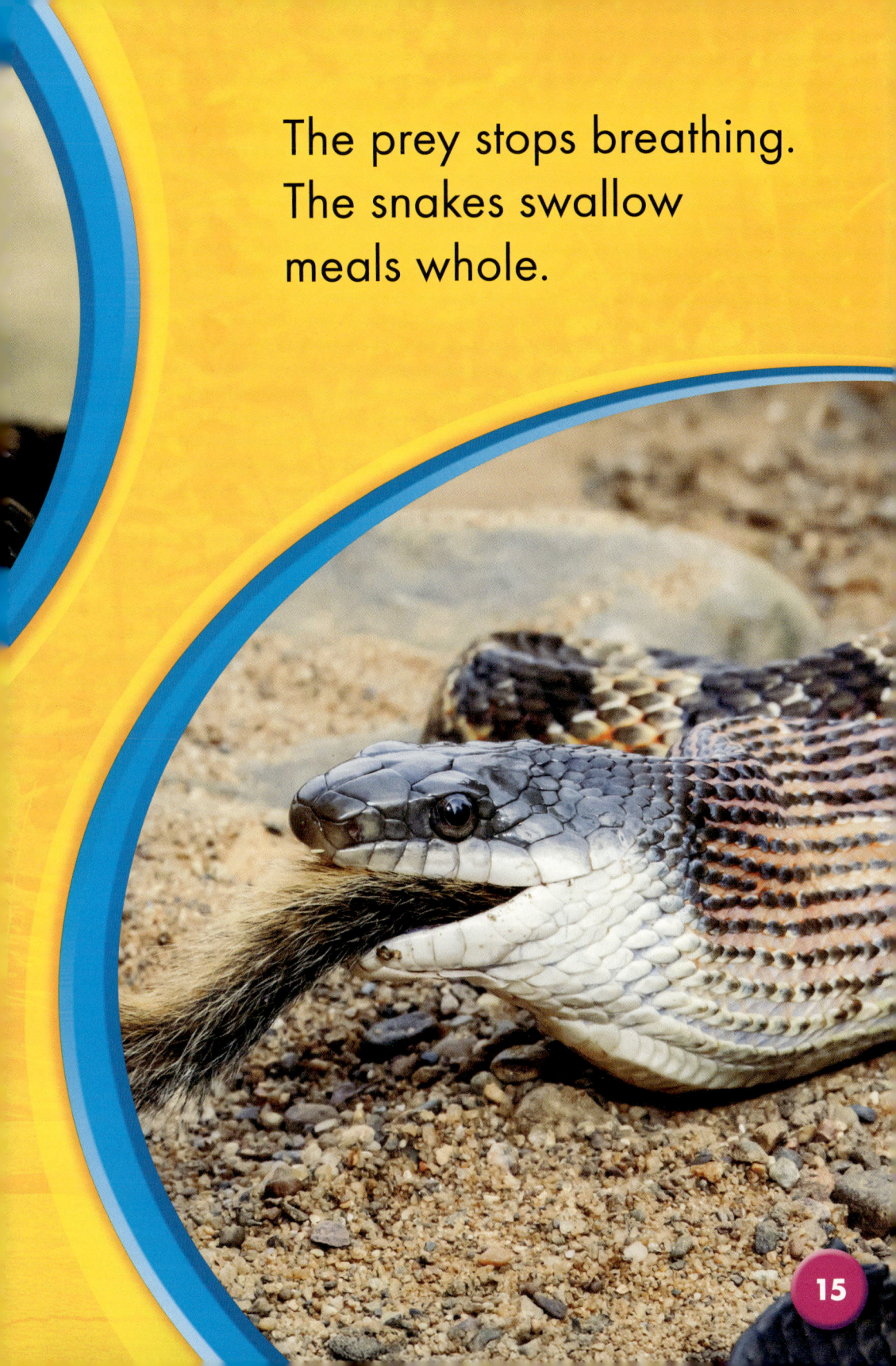

15

Hawks, foxes, and other snakes eat young rat snakes.

predator

Rat snakes give off a stinky smell. This often scares away **predators**.

From Babies to Adults

eggs

Female rat snakes lay many eggs. Some species lay up to 30 eggs!

Female snakes leave the eggs.
About two months later,
the eggs **hatch**.

19

Young rat snakes
care for themselves.
The snakes are adults
after around three years.

Adult rat snakes like
to live alone. They are
important predators!

Eastern Rat Snake Stats

status in the wild: least concern

life span: about 20 years

21

Glossary

constrictors—snakes that squeeze prey

grasslands—lands covered with grasses and other soft plants with few bushes or trees

hatch—to break open

predators—animals that hunt other animals for food

prey—animals that are hunted by other animals for food

reptiles—cold-blooded animals that have backbones and lay eggs

ridge—a part that stands taller than other parts of a surface

rodents—small animals that gnaw on their food

scales—thin plates that cover and protect an animal's body

snouts—the noses and mouths of some animals

species—kinds of animals

wrap—to cover by winding around

To Learn More

AT THE LIBRARY

Mattern, Joanne. *Corn Snakes*. Minneapolis, Minn.:
Bellwether Media, 2025.

Mattern, Joanne. *Pythons*. Minneapolis, Minn.:
Bellwether Media, 2026.

Nguyen, Suzane. *Boa Constrictors*. Minneapolis, Minn.:
Bellwether Media, 2025.

ON THE WEB

Factsurfer.com gives you
a safe, fun way to find
more information.

1. Go to www.factsurfer.com.

2. Enter "rat snakes" into the search box
   and click 🔍.

3. Select your book cover to see a list
   of related content.

Index

The images in this book are reproduced through the courtesy of: dwi putra stock, front cover (snake), p. 11; Rudiant_axer, front cover (background); Chase D'animulls, p. 3; Mike Wilhelm, p. 4; Wileydoc, p. 7; E.R. Degginger/ Alamy, pp. 8, 19; Lauren Suryanata, pp. 9, 23; Jean Blom, p. 10; Prajjwal Ray, p. 11 (inset); TinkerJulie, p. 12; Michelle Gilders/ Alamy, pp. 12-13, 15; Raseduly, p. 13 (bullfrog); Jesus Cobaleda, p. 13 (rat); Ihor Hvozdetskyi, p. 13 (mouse); Connect Images/ Alamy, p. 14; David Brace, p. 16; Ton Ponchai, p. 17; McDonald Wildlife Photography Inc./ Getty, p. 18; Robert Hamilton/ Alamy, pp. 20, 20-21.